Dales Traverse

By the same author:
AINSTY BOUNDS WALK

Dales Traverse

A 25-mile circular challenge walk in Upper Wharfedale

by
Simon Townson

Dalesman Books
1984

The Dalesman Publishing Company Ltd.,
Clapham, via Lancaster LA2 8EB

First published 1984

ISBN: 0 85206 787 9

Printed by Alf Smith & Co., Bradford.

Contents

Cover photograph of Arncliffe, Littondale, by S. C. Sedgwick.

Maps on pages 14-22 by Hazel Chester.

Drawings in the text by Stanley Bond, E. C. Clark, V. Hill, Claude Horsfall, E. Jeffrey, J. C. Longstaff, Den Oldroyd, J. Owram, D. C. Smith and T. Stead.

N
W
E
S
DALES TRAVERSE

Introduction

THE idea of this long distance walk came to me when I saw problems on the Three Peaks with footpath erosion and I thought it was time to take pressure off the walk. The Dales Traverse was launched; it was going to be a tough walk of 25 miles with a time limit to give a challenge to walkers. The inaugural walk was on May 22, 1983, by 306 people.

The Dales Traverse shows some of the most interesting views of the Yorkshire Dales, as you walk along Hill Castle Scar to Kettlewell. The tedious ascent of Top Mere Road can be enlivened by looking back at intervals as the view down Wharfedale unfolds, and also by identifying the evidence of former lead mining, including spoil heaps, shafts, "hushes" (ravines excavated to impound streams to flush out the ore) and a flue built up the hillside from the old smelt mill in Cam Gill. Top Mere Road was used daily by miners with their pack ponies and wagons. Buckden Pike (2,302ft.) itself gives you a splended view of the walk you are enjoying.

The main sponsor of the walk is Wheatfields Hospice in Leeds, a special home for cancer patients. For every badge and certificate sold, a small part goes to the Hospice.

Those who complete the walk may apply for a Certificate (20p), Badge (80p) by sending a stamped addressed envelope 9in. x 6½in. and report with details of date, direction and time; there is a 12 hour time limit.

Apply to:
Mr. S. Townson
18 Victoria Street
Wetherby
West Yorkshire LS22 4RE

Cheques and postal orders to be made payable to Wheatfields Hospice, please.

The Route

Kilnsey to Kettlewell

The Dales Traverse starts in the Wharfedale village of Kilnsey, under the imposing Kilnsey Crag (974679). Take the main road south from the village and after 500 yds. turn left to Conistone on the opposite side of the valley. Head north out of the village, taking the first track on the right, climb up to Wassa Hill and on to the top of Hill Castle Scar (at 991682). Walk north along the Scar towards Kettlewell, noting the view up Littondale to the west. After about 1½ miles, join the track which comes in from your left through the gate into the wood (982706) and follow it down to the road.

Proceed north along the road and at 972721 take the farm track on the right which leads to Kettlewell passing the church on the left.

Kettlewell to Buckden

The next section from Kettlewell village has a long hard pull up to Buckden Pike. From the village shop and post office, you take the Coverdale road opposite, for about 600 yds. till you come to the track on the left up to Cam Head. The tedious ascent of Top Mere Road can be enlivened by looking back at intervals as the view down Wharfedale unfolds. Continue up the track till you reach the Starbotton road, turn left at footpath sign, go through two gates with stiles then turn right through wall opening. Continue up the track till you come to a bend. Just after it and before the fence turn right to the corner of the wall. Follow the wall for a short while till you come to a fence-type gate, go over and turn left, to follow the wall which takes you up to Top Mere Top. Continue following the wall **(Please do not take stones off the walls on this section of the walk which is very wet in places)** to Buckden Pike, passing a memorial cross which commemorates the death of five Polish airmen whose plane crashed nearby in bad weather in January 1942.

Buckden Pike, because of its height, gives an extensive view, though much of the nearer lower ground is hidden. Langstrothdale and Waldendale are however seen to good advantage. The Three Peaks can be seen also. Whernside and Great Shunner Fell stand out in clear weather.

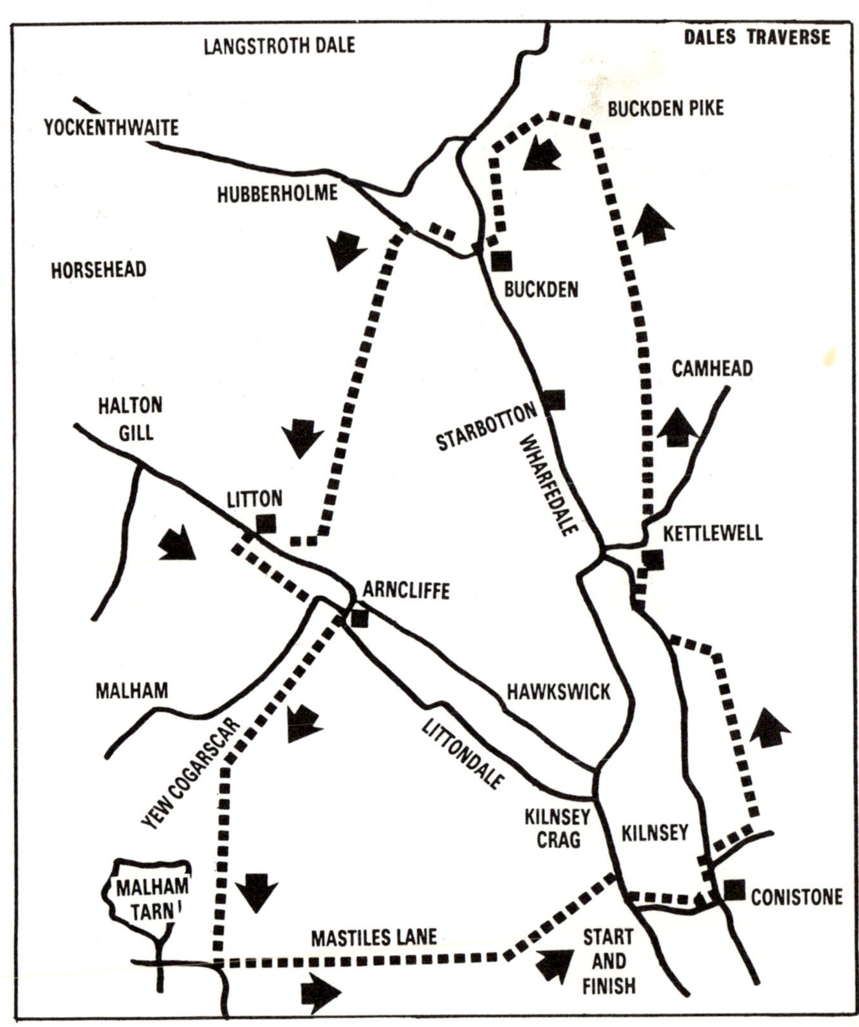
DALES TRAVERSE
LANGSTROTH DALE
YOCKENTHWAITE
BUCKDEN PIKE
HUBBERHOLME
HORSEHEAD
BUCKDEN
CAMHEAD
HALTON
GILL
STARBOTTON
WHARFEDALE
LITTON
KETTLEWELL
ARNCLIFFE
MALHAM
HAWKSWICK
YEW COGARSCAR
LITTONDALE
KILNSEY
CRAG
KILNSEY
MALHAM
TARN
CONISTONE
MASTILES LANE
START
AND
FINISH

From the trig point you then follow the wall on the right down after about 400 yards, bear left for a short while, then right to a gate which takes you to a track down to Buckden Rake. Turn left and follow it all the way down to Buckden village. Looking across the valley you can see the next section of the walk.

Buckden to Arncliffe

From the village you take the Hubberholme road for about 600 yds. to the track on the left which goes to Redmire Farm. Just before the farm you will see a footpath sign on your right. This takes you over to Litton passing Redmire Pot on your left (933766); again this is a hard climb but the view from the top in good weather is marvellous. From the trig point (926748) the path becomes easy down to Litton passing the *Queen's Arms*.

Turn right on the main road for a few yards to the footpath on the left which goes over the footbridge. Turn left along the river to East Garth then follow the footpath to Arncliffe village.

Arncliffe to Kilnsey

At the *Falcon Inn* you take the footpath over to Malham passing Yew Cogar Scar. Take note of the view as you go along, especially the small cairns along the path to Middle House. Follow track through to gate (907678), then to wire fence over stile and along farm track to Street Gate (905656), passing West Great Scar on right. At Street Gate, turn left and follow the ancient Mastiles Lane, a former drovers' road, east over Gordale Back. Walk along Mastiles to Mastiles Gate, then start to climb over Kilnsey Moor, from which you will now have a good view of the finish and the area you have just walked. Go past the quarry on the left into Kilnsey to the finish.

ARNCLIFFE VILLAGE

Maps of the Route

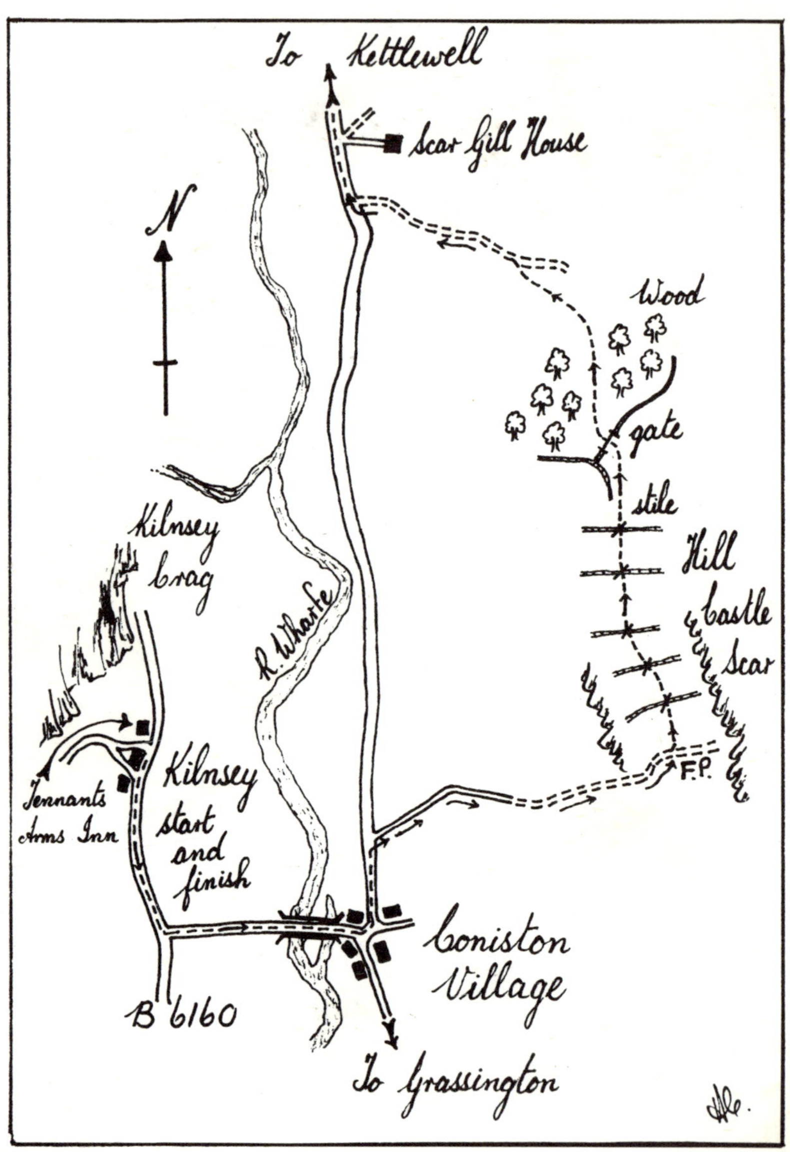
To Kettlewell
Scar Gill House
N
Wood
gate
stile
Hill
Castle
Scar
F.P.
Kilnsey
Crag
R. Wharfe
Kilnsey
start
and
finish
Tennants
Arms Inn
Coniston
Village
B 6160
To Grassington

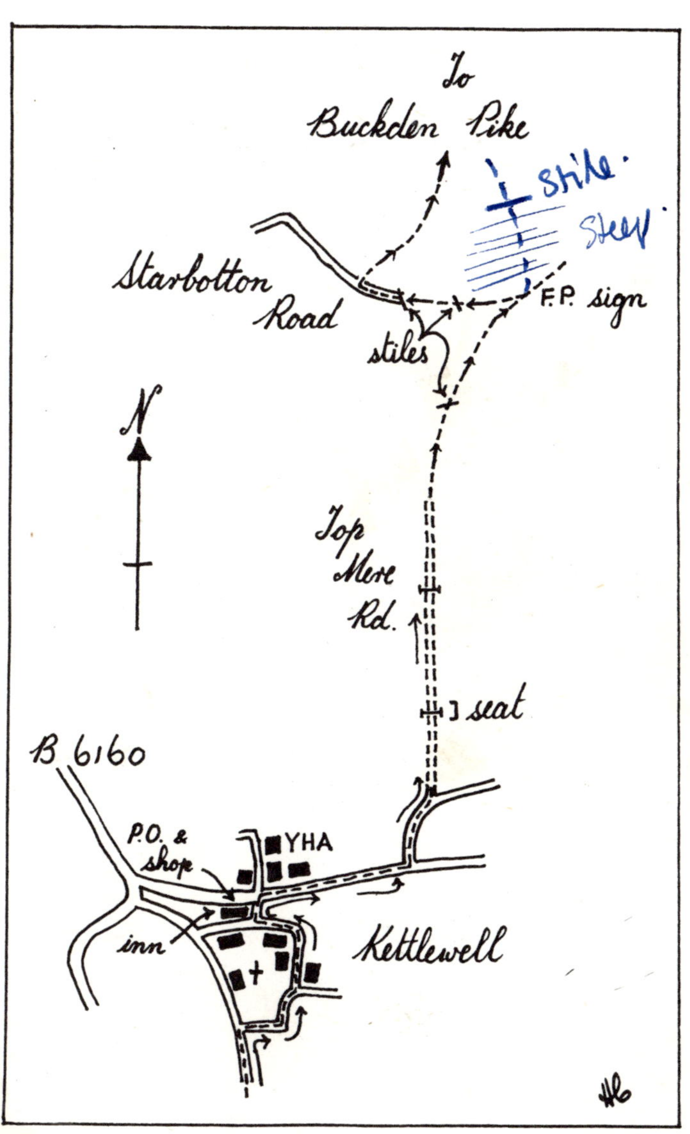
To
Buckden Pike
Stile.
Steep.
Starbotton
Road
F.P. sign
stiles
N
Top
Mere
Rd.
seat
B 6160
P.O. &
shop
YHA
inn
Kettlewell
HG

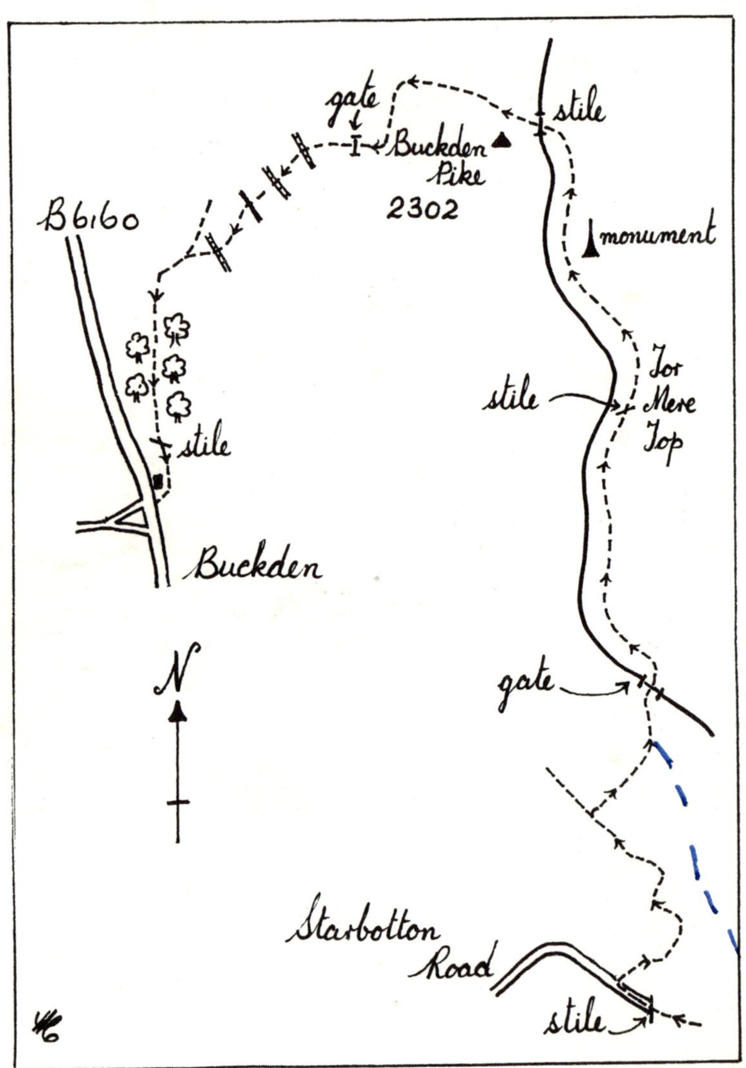
gate
stile
Buckden
Pike
2302
B6160
monument
Tor
Mere
Top
stile
stile
Buckden
N
gate
Starbotton
Road
stile

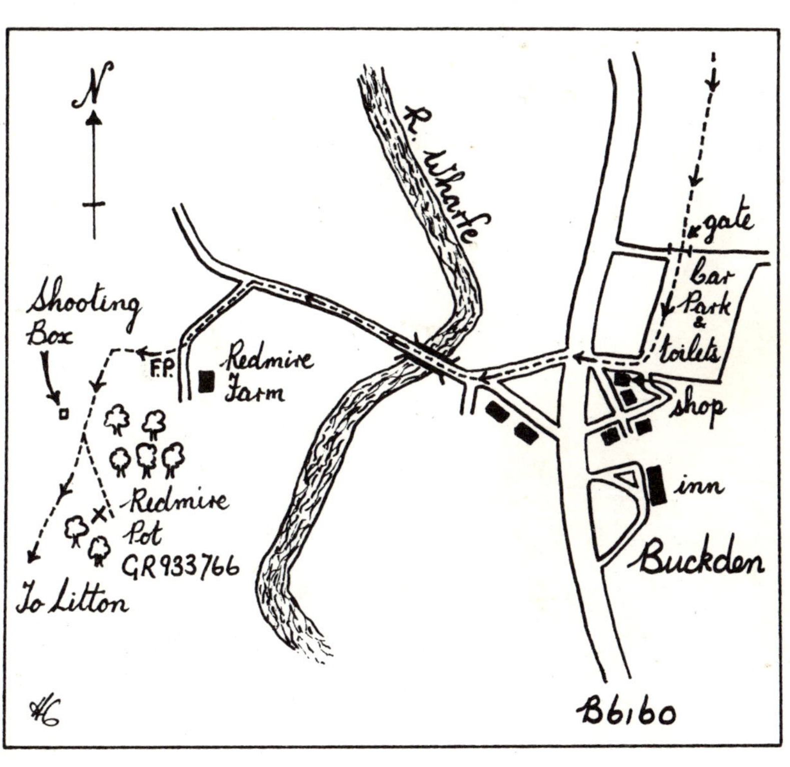
N
R. Wharfe
gate
Car
Park
&
toilets
Shooting
Box
F.P.
Redmire
Farm
shop
inn
Redmire
Pot
GR933766
Buckden
To Litton
B6160

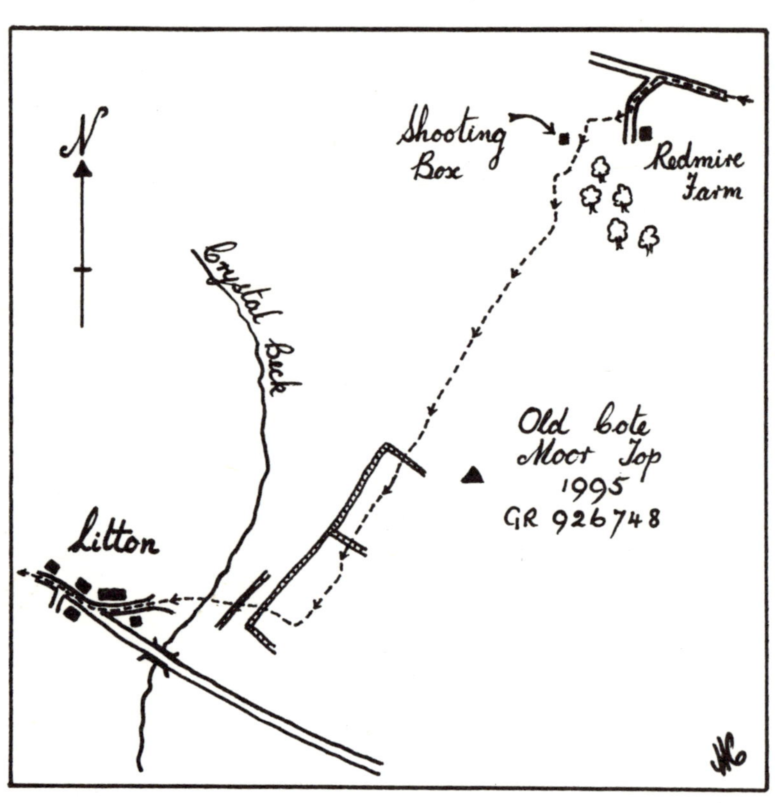
N
Shooting Box
Redmire Farm
Crystal Beck
Old Cote Moor Top
1995
GR 926748
Litton

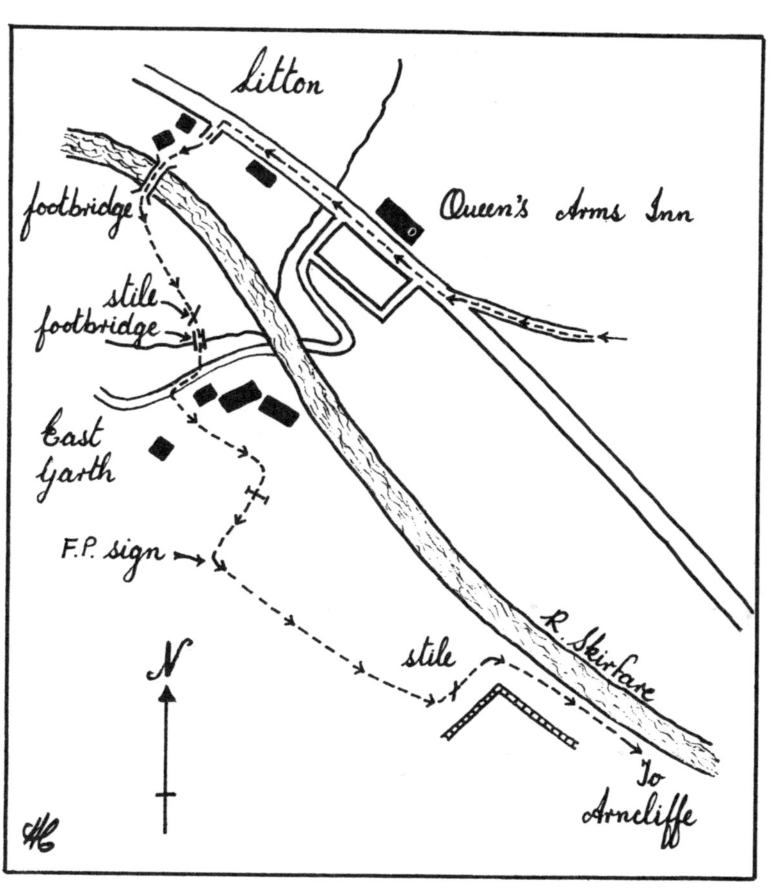
Litton
Queen's Arms Inn
footbridge
stile
footbridge
East
Garth
F.P. sign
N
stile
R. Skirfare
To
Arncliffe

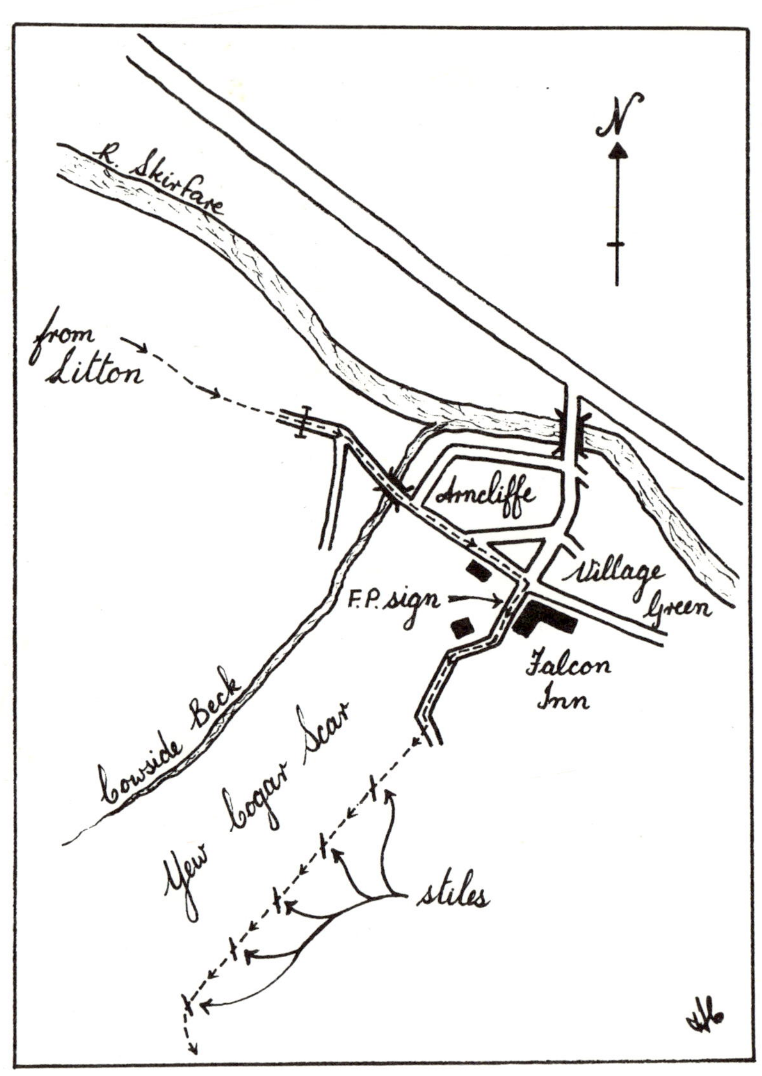
N
R. Skirfare
from Litton
Arncliffe
Village Green
F.P. sign
Falcon Inn
Cowside Beck
Yew Cogar Scar
stiles

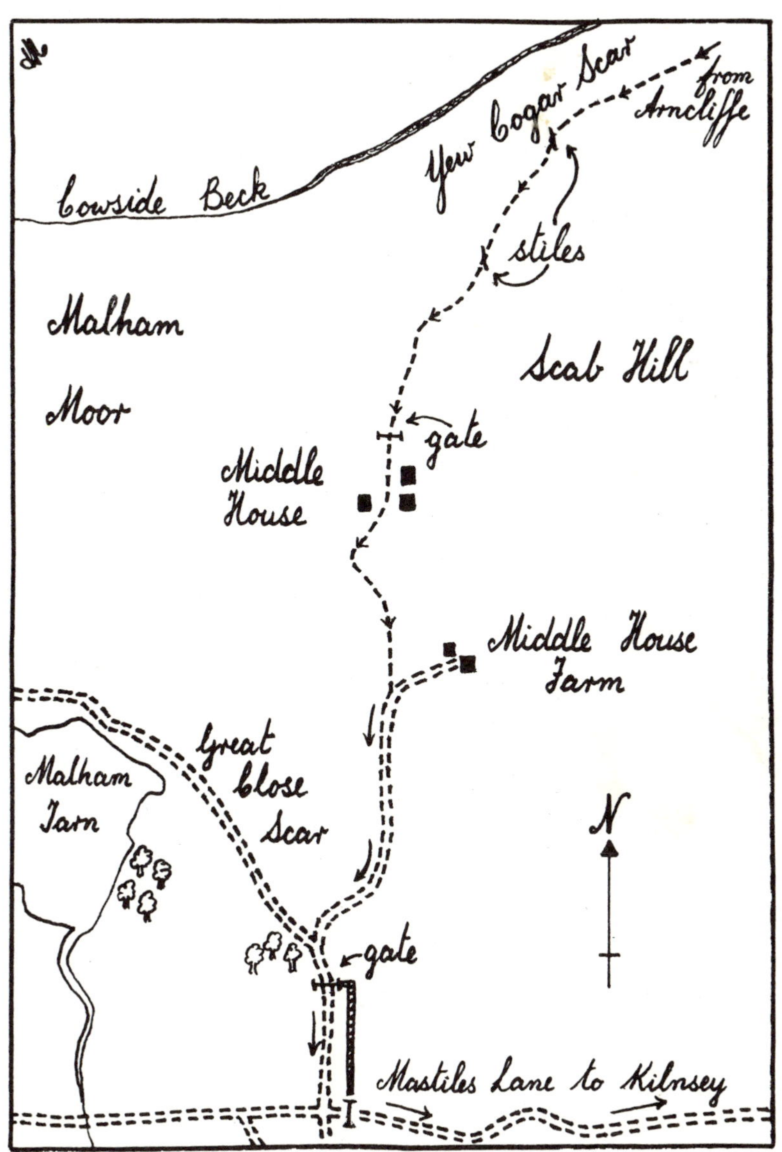
Cowside Beck
Yew Cogar Scar
from Arncliffe
stiles
Malham Moor
Scab Hill
gate
Middle House
Middle House Farm
Great Close Scar
Malham Tarn
N
gate
Mastiles Lane to Kilnsey

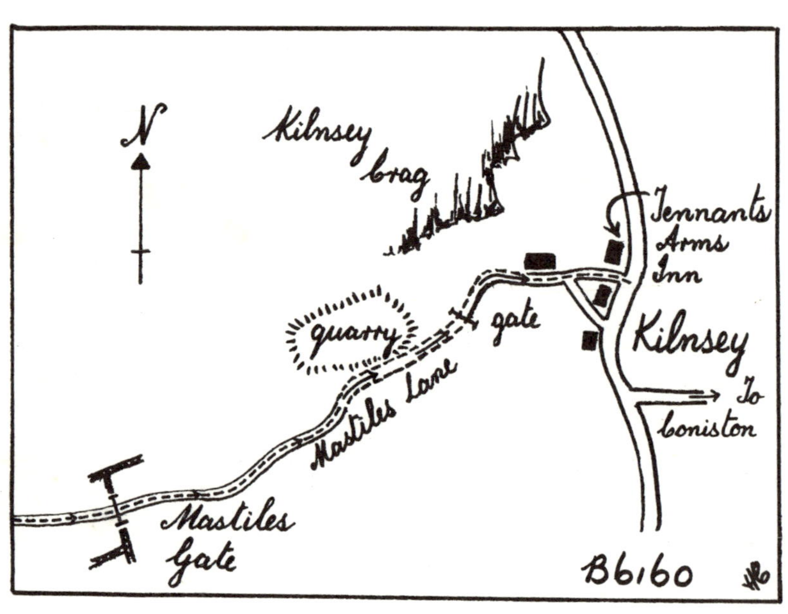
N
Kilnsey Crag
Tennants Arms Inn
quarry
gate
Kilnsey
To Coniston
Mastiles Lane
Mastiles Gate
B6160

Wharfedale

WHARFEDALE is a valley favoured by nature and enriched by romance. The narrow dale, cut by a crystal river and shut in by rolling pastures and sombre fells, has had beauty showered on it lavishly; and in it ancient men, monks, shepherds, craftsmen and yeomen have woven its story. To many it has stood and stands as the spot in England 'beloved over all'.

It lies in Craven, cut off from Wensleydale and Swaledale not only by the fells but by the stronger though invisible boundary of a former Riding and a District. The people of Lower Wharfedale and Craven speak of the higher dale and its branch of Littondale as 'the dales'. As high up as Grassington, if the river rises suddenly in fine weather a farmer will say: 'Ther' must 'a' bin some rain up i' t' dales.' The term, which must be very old, is used without any thought of the other Pennine dales. It has arisen because the valley is divided naturally by a bend or a rise into separate stretches, each with characteristic features and each so different that going from one to another is like entering another valley. Some have names of their own, such as Langstrothdale and the old districts of Kettlewelldale and Barden Chase. The divisions have led lovers of the valley to find the particular corner which for them is Wharfedale, and let the rest be a background to it.

The river flowing through these changes is the chief connecting link. The Wharfe is the most approachable of dale rivers; for miles the road runs beside it, crossing and recrossing it, and nearly all the way there are paths along its banks. It starts among wild fells beyond which tower the giants of the Yorkshire Pennines, Whernside, Ingleborough, and Penyghent. At Beckermonds it is met by the Greenfield Beck, and then flows as a rocky stream through the dramatic valley of Langstrothdale. Here along the steep hillsides are scattered grey farms and weathered hamlets, and at Hubberholme, close beside the river, an ancient church.

Innumerable becks and rills drain into it, so that by the time it reaches Buckden, its first village, it has the breadth and power of a growing river; but the dale is still narrow, and the meadows stretch

only a short way between the river and the fells. Below Kettlewell it is joined by the river Skirfare from Littondale, and the flat valley, once the bed of a lake, is dominated by the enormous overhanging cliff of Kilnsey Crag. Another bed, and the valley is a green basin in the limestone pastures, cut with white walls, and with the town of Grassington giving it life. Below Burnsall the river banks are overhung with trees, there is richer colouring to the hills, and the villages and walls are brown. Through them the river flows to the magnificence of the wooded country round Barden Tower and Bolton Abbey.

It is a favourite river of anglers, yielding as it does grayling and some of the largest trout in the North of England. On most days in the season men can be seen motionless on the banks or wading up to the thighs fishing. Standing patiently there, they seem to have cast off the

FARMHOUSES IN LITTONDALE

rush and flurry of the times, as they listen to the tale the river tells of the weather it has left behind in the hills which gave it birth.

Trees add their share to the beauty of the valley. They are everywhere; by the river banks, up the gills, in the meadows. They range from the stunted bushes, relics of the old forest, which cover the steep hillside like the thinning hair on an old man's head, to the giants of their kind which give richness to the lower dale. A farmer in Littondale in the middle of the last century said: 'I can tell of the time when a squirrel could hop all the way from Foxup to Kilnsey without touching the ground once'; and a similar saying would be true of the bigger dale.

Enclosing it all are the fells, long ridges broken only by gills, but rising in places to individual peaks, like the crouching shapes of Buckden Pike and Penyghent, the lordly mass of Great Whernside, the rock-covered summit of Simon's Seat. They have a more intimate quality than the loftier fells of the Lake District. Their expanse and steadfastness bring repose to the soul. They are the rain-bringers, for they belong to the clouds as much as to the earth, but they bring, too,

Kettlewell

a calm which is stored up in them for ever, and which they give out perhaps on a still evening or after a mighty storm to those who can take it. They make Wharfedale, particularly in its upper part, a walker's country. You can climb them, and get from each its particular view; you can cross them into other dales; but you can never exhaust them. They are friendly hills, but in snow or mist or darkness you can lose your way on them in five minutes.

By far the largest part of Wharfedale is pastoral, a shepherds' country. The words heard most frequently in the dale are 'sheep' and 'pastures.' The pastures sweep from the meadows to the unenclosed fells, which are generally called 'the moor', and are vast, rolling stretches, in their breadth and space as open as moors, but covered with grass. They owe this rich grass, which makes some of the finest summer grazing in England, to the limestone, which grows grass instead of the heather and rushes of millstone grit.

The Craven Fault, which enters the dale above Threshfield, crosses it below Burnsall, and dies out in Nidderdale, marks the line between these two formations. On one side of it, where the millstone grit has dropped, there are heather moors and brown rocks, and on the other, where the millstone grit cap has worn away leaving a limestone summit, there are pastures and grey rock.

Like all limestone country, this abounds in underground rivers and caves. The gaping entrances to the caves show the exposed limestone, as do the jutting crags of Kilnsey and Arncliffe, the scars which break through the hills like ramparts of castles, and the bared pavements, often called 'clowders', on the ridges.

The walls which cut the pastures and meadows are of stone quarried from these hills. The white walls of Wharfedale are some of the things you remember most about it, bulging dipping walls, their crevices a rooting place for ferns and flowers. They line the roads, start tracks up the fells, border the meadows, curl round tiny garths, make jigsaw patterns above the villages, and strike out in bold lines over the pastures. Their builders seem to have loved the material with which they worked, and used it as much as they could. Bleached and weathered by sun and storms, they take the colour of the day, showing grey in sombre weather and dazzlingly white in the sunshine. They are a part of their surroundings, and in perfect harmony with them. Winding with the roads, they unite them to the valley and the hills.

The older buildings are of limestone too. Conistone seen from across the valley and Kilnsey from the lane above are striking examples of the stone which belongs to a district being the right one for building on it. Many of the villages cluster in what seems a dangerous

fashion at the foot of gills, and the houses look as though they had fallen from the scars behind.

It is to the limestone that Wharfedale owes its wealth of wild flowers, making it a treasure-house for naturalists. They are an accompaniment to every walk, the Alpine flowers, relics of a pre-glacial flora; the lilies of the valley giving out their heavy fragrance in the Grassington and Hawkswick woods; the colourful meadow flowers before the grass is cut for hay. The common ones are larger and more splendid here, and everywhere there are rare varieties to be found for the seeking. But the flower which seems to belong most to Wharfedale is the mealy primrose. The bright, cheery bunches of blossom on their long stems, blooming for a few weeks between the spring show and the summer pageant, and giving a rosy haze to the gills and lower slopes on which they flourish, are unforgettable.

This is the valley as we see it to-day. Artists have painted it and made it their home. Poets have sung of it, and so added glamour to it. But there is an indefinable sadness in its beauty, a kind of melancholy, as if the memory hung over it of things which have been and are not any more.Sometimes the dale seems to wait and listen, as if it heard echoes of that fuller life and the people who made it.

The shapes of their dwellings and square fields, their burial circles and mounds can be seen; and flint and stone implements which they made and used are found in mole hills and rabbit scrapes. An echo of their presence hangs over their settlements, a feeling even in the loneliest places of the work of man. As many as two hundred prehistoric sites have been traced, and it seems possible that the dale would be as thickly populated in the Iron Age, which began here about 300 BC, as it is now. Often the modern village in the valley is just below the old village on the hills, as at Grassington and Arncliffe.

Signs of a road and a fort are left of the Romans. Cultivation terraces on the hillsides and fragments of crosses remain from the Angles; and they and the Danes named the villages. The Normans enclosed the forests for their hunting and increased the cultivation.

During four centuries the monks were a powerful influence in the dale. Bolton Abbey held property in it, but the largest owners were

KILNSEY OLD HALL

KETTLEWELL YOUTH HOSTEL

the monks of Fountains Abbey — most of Littondale and Langstrothdale and vast tracks round Kilnsey belonged to them, being part of the hundred square miles of land which they owned in Craven.

Early in its history men had dug for lead here as they did in the other Yorkshire dales. Signs of their workings, from the shallow diggings of the first searches to the deep shafts and levels of the last, are scattered over the fells. The industry was vigorous all over the dale; there were smelt mills on the becks behind many of the villages, but it was most extensive round Grassington. There was a mining tradition here passed down from one generation to another for centuries and following laws similar to those of the Romans. From the middle of the seventeenth century the mineral rights were owned by the Earls of Burlington who also worked the mines. With the development of the industry in the nineteenth century enormous profits were made.

Along with these went other industries. There were the millers grinding corn with no thought that there would come a day when no corn would be grown or ground in the dale; the wallers, who were very powerful men, building walls round the new enclosures; the shoemakers centred at Thorpe, fitting shoes for the monks and then for the dalespeople; the tailors sitting cross-legged as they sewed in farmhouse kitchens.

The daily happenings of the valley with its customs and superstitions come crowding back. There is Nan, the witch of Kilnsey, tramping to Skipton market a hundred years ago with a guinea-pig under her arm to aid her in her spells, striking terror in the people who long retained the belief in fairies inherited from their Celtic ancestors. A wagon piled high with besoms made in Threshfield rumbles past her on the road.

'Yan, tan, tether, pether, pimp' sounds from a farmyard as shepherds count their sheep with Celtic numerals. It is Sunday morning in Langstrothdale fifty years ago, and a procession gathered from the remote farms and hamlets winds down the long road by the river to Hubberholme church, the bright dresses of the women making a line of colour between the sombre fells. A Littondale shepherd places a twig at a particular place on the moor so that its shadow cast by the sun shall tell him when it is time to go home.

Through all these phases the country has altered comparatively little. Its feeling of constancy is so strong that each season as it comes seems permanent. When the larches are spreading their new green against the darker fir trees, blackthorns are bursting with blossom before they have had time to leaf, and primroses and violets are poking up on the banks and hills, it seems that it will always be spring here. When summer brings her green to woods and hills, and her more exotic flowers to the meadows, you feel that it must last for ever. There is an impression of change when autumn with its golden glory comes, and bracken flames on the hills, and trees vie in colouring, growing in vividness with each day, so that there is about it all the startling quality of a sunset. But when winter trees show the beauty of naked branches, and the snow-covered valley is a picture in black and white, the only colour a faint glow which reddens the hills for a few brief moments as the sun sinks, the sense of permanence is deep again. There are few more satisfying experiences than to watch the pageant of the seasons through the dale.

Villages of Upper Wharfedale

Conistone

Conistone stands on the east bank of the river, and its antiquity reaches back to pre-historic times, as the remains of man found in the tumuli in Conistone pastures abundantly testify. The Norman historic period is grandly typified in the pillars and arches of its ancient church, whose foundations probably date back to the western or Celtic religious influence. If we could lift the curtain which hides the past, many a stirring scene and gathering of bygone people, peasant and monk, should we witness in and around this old kirkyard. There are several 17th century houses bearing dates, and a green and maypole. The hill overlooking the village is called 'Coniston Pie' — the crust and contents would doubtless be found not over tender eating! A cleft in the hill goes by the name of 'Gurling Trough'. This village was famed in the past for Whangby (tough skimmed milk) cheese and bread.

Kilnsey

The hamlet of Kilnsey, overshadowed by its rock, is on the opposite side of the Wharfe. Here there were two inns, *The Anglers* and *The Tennant Arms*. It was from the *Anglers' Arms*, which has now long gone, that Dr. Petty rode forth on that dark night more than a century ago to meet his death at the hands of Tom Lee. There where the old gate stood, at the entrance to the wood, the murderer lay silently crouching in ambush for the advent of his victim, since the doctor knew too much of Tom Lee's evil doings for anything but his death to satisfy. For some time it almost appeared as though Lee would escape the hands of justice, but evil will out. His bones long rattled on the gibbet near the scene of the murder.

CONISTONE BRIDGE

How unpretending the hamlet appears by contrast with the fore-headed crag, 170 feet high, that overshadows it. Ages ago some relentless grinding force, the ice flow of a melting glacier, under-carved and scored its Sphinx-like profile. To-day jackdaws and rock-dove nest in its niches. From the rock spring several fountains of the clearest sparkling water which form a beautiful stream; its banks along the face of the cliff are fringed with marsh marigolds, lending a touch of strong colour contrasting with the sombre bleached grey of the stupendous cliff rising wall-like overhead.

Kettlewell

Kettlewell stands in the apex of land between two streams, and at the foot of the pass leading from here into Coverdale. Sheer above on every hand rise the hills canopied by the clouds. The wall of high hills has to some extent preserved the old traditions and customs which have been handed down from generations of forefathers born, bred and dying under the shadow of the everlasting hills, The dalesmen here are a fusion of three races, Celt, Saxon and Norse.

KETTLEWELL VILLAGE

There are three inns at Kettlewell — The Racehorses, Blue Bell, and King's Head — and much other accommodation for visitors. On the green is the maypole and the stumps of the old stocks still remain. One striking feature at Kettlewell which one sees and hears almost at every turn is water. It comes swirling from dark ravines in the hills, leaping and surging under bridges and over boulders, washing the walls of the houses in its wild madcap course from the hills. There are a few houses which date back to the late Tudor and early Jacobean period — thick walls, mullioned windows and stoutly timbered frames.

The church has a very old foundation, but little remains of the original building which was demolished in 1820, the worst period in the history of church architecture for such a thing to have occurred, but the deed then done is beyond all human remedy. With the exception of a few fragments, the only relic of the same age as the early church is the large Norman font ornamented with three boars' heads. This vessel alone will repay a visit. During the late restoration the interior of the church was finished with sound taste and judgement.

East and north of the village are Langcliffe, Dowbergill, Douka Cave, Scala Park and the pass into Coverdale. Douka Cave is situated near East Scala Park in Aynham's pastures at the head of a deep ravine.

Buckden

The first village on the Wharfe lies at a point where three ways meet — the road from Langstrothdale, the road down the dale, and the road through Cray and over the Kidstones Pass into Wensleydale. Perched on the hillside at this junction, the village has a slightly bewildered air as if it does not quite know which it is, a centre to which the life of the upper dale is drawn, a goal to be reached from lower down, or a starting-point for the pass.

The little village with its sloping green crouches at the foot of the gill under the bulwark of Buckden Pike. It is an elusive place, retreating into narrow byways which must be explored to find how large it really is. It has the first village hall, and the first shop, which is also the post office, in the dale. How many walkers must have opened the door of this tiny shop and heard its clanging bell as they went in to buy chocolate before starting out for the Stake or Kidstones Passes, to climb Buckden Pike, cross the fells into Littondale, or take the road up Langstrothdale!

BUCKDEN BRIDGE AND VILLAGE

There were once three inns here. The *Low Cock,* the first to disappear, was in a yard opposite Buckden House. The white house up a lane at the top end of the village was the *High Cock*. The *Buck Inn* remains, standing back from the road with a prosperous air, and forming a centre for the comings and goings of the village.

Buckden is a starting-point for walkers. Any direction gives, practically from the beginning, those individual pictures which are one of the joys of Wharfedale — a glimpse through trees of hill and stream which might be Switzerland; fir trees climbing a ravine as in some Scottish scene; a little triangle of the grey roofs of Buckden; a view from across the valley of the village at the foot of the gill. Each way brings a sense of freedom and escape.

Litton

The 'village on a torrent', from the Old English Hlydan-tun, straggles round the base of the jutting fell called Middlemoor which divides Sawyer's Gill from Pott's Gill. The grey village clings to the slope, as if afraid that one of the two gills would draw it up into its fastnesses. Its houses lining the road with solid dignity are early eighteenth rather than the usual seventeenth century.

The Buckden track joins the road by the house which has been the inn since 1842. The original inn, down a grassy lane between the road and the river, is now a barn. At the end of the eighteenth century the landlord was Christopher, always known as Kitty, Mytton, a blacksmith, but it was last kept by an old woman called Mrs Taylor. She avoided paying for a licence by selling penny and halfpenny parkins and giving beer or ale with them. Until 1842, when a bridge was made beyond the village, the inn lay on the road to Settle which forded the river just below.

Arncliffe

At Arncliffe the Skirface is joined by Cowside Beck, which comes swirling and leaping out of its prisoned spring in Fountain Fell. In its race through the wild hills it passes Darnbrook, a farmhouse immortalized by the pen of Wordsworth and by the brushes of Birket and Gilbert Foster. Arncliffe is very charming, a gem in a ring of wild hills. The church, in its picturesque environment of trees and the brown moorland stream surging through the emerald dale, forms an interesting subject. The Norman church built in the 11th century came to an end in the 15th century and the present church was restored and beautified in 1841.

RIVER SKIRFARE, ARNCLIFFE

Footpaths

FORMER landowners and a short-sighted policy has made the 'public footpath' definition of very little use. The important point to remember is the reason for this controversial subject. It is realised by only too few residents and visitors to the countryside that the land is the livelihood of the farmer, and a great deal of damage can be done by the thoughtless actions of people unused to the countryside — walking through meadows, the breaking of fences and hedges, gates left open which were shut, stone walls knocked down. These are only a few small items in themselves, but they cause pounds worth of damage to the farmers and landowners, destroying the crops, mixing animals that should be segregated, and spoiling the amenities of the countryside which is everyone's heritage.

A few of the moorland routes are on indefinite paths, or paths that are not easily followed at first acquaintance. Others are on paths which are disputed by land agents, often plastered with "No Road" (which does not mean "No Footpath") or "Trespassers will be prosecuted" (which is not acknowledged by English law without damage). Here again, civility and appreciation of the other man's view if challenged should lead the way to an understanding on both sides.

Useful Information

FOR the walker en route there are plenty of refreshment stops. Kettlewell has a good selection of pubs and places to eat. Buckden is about the same. For those who have to stick to a time limit it is best to try to avoid all the pubs en route!

There is a good bus service from Grassington during the summer months. To find out how often they run, a timetable of the buses is available at National Park Centres. The Centres are located at:-

Grassington (752748)
Malham (Tel: Airton 363)

Maps required en route are:-

1:50,000 sheet 98 "Wensleydale and Wharfedale"
1:25,000 "Malham and Upper Wharfedale"

Accommodation

THERE are three Youth Hostels very close to the walk. They are:

Kettlewell (Tel: 075676 232)
Linton (Tel: 0756 752400)
Malham (Tel: 07293 321)

Also, there are plenty of bed and breakfast stops very close to the walk, especially at the start. The *Tennant Arms* has accommodation and cottages for large parties at the start of the walk (see below).

Again, if you ring the National Park Centres they will help you.

Tennant Arms Hotel

THE *Tennant Arms Hotel* is situated in Upper Wharfedale where Mastiles Lane joins the Kettlewell to Skipton road at the hamlet of Kilnsey. The hotel is dwarfed by the magnificent Kilnsey Crag and is a very popular spot with both walkers and tourists alike. There has been a hostelry on this site since at least the 17th century and during the past few years it has been converted to meet the needs of the 1980s.

There is a large flag-stoned bar where you can refresh yourself from a large selection of real ales and bottled wines. The bar meal menu is very varied with both hot and cold dishes and the house speciality is an excellent salad bar. The hotel is extensively used by walkers who are just pausing for a break on the daily journey or are using the hotel as a base to explore the surrounding dale countryside. The accommodation is comfortable and up to date with all rooms having their own bathroom and toilet, fully carpeted and centrally heated with colour TV and tea and coffee-making facilities available.

You will find that the hotel management are enthusiastic walkers and were very pleased that the hotel has been selected as the start and finish point for the newly introduced Dales Traverse walk.

Special note: Do not park in front of the hotel when doing the walk as the space is needed for guests paying a short visit. Please park opposite on the space by the side of the beck.

KETTLEWELL AND GREAT WHERNSIDE

WHEATFIELDS

Wheatfields Hospice

WHEATFIELDS Hospice provides continuing care for patients with advanced cancer. A large number of patients dying from cancer suffer unnecessarliy because there are not places in hospitals or the facilities at home to care for them. Many of us have known those who could have been helped in the last few months of life if a suitable home had existed providing nursing and medical care, where friends and relatives were always welcome and where there was comfort and peace.

In a lovely old Victorian house surrounded by beautiful landscaped gardens the highly skilled staff of Wheatfields give this very special care in an atmosphere of cheerfulness and dignity. At Wheatfields relatives and friends also receive unique support and understanding at this difficult time.

Care is always possible even if there is no cure and Wheatfields is available for anyone in need of short term care. Many patients are admitted temporarily for the relief of pain and other symptoms, and often to give a break to those caring for them, and as a result some patients are able to return home.

Acknowledgements

I WOULD like to thank all who have given me material to put this book together, especially my wife Elaine who did all the typing, but the reason why I devised this walk is to give all who enjoy walking the fells the pleasure of knowing that the money that is made from the badge and certificates plus the sale of this book will go to help cancer patients who spend their time at Wheatfields Hospice. Please give generously and:

Thank You

S. Townson

Books for Walkers

Ainsty Bounds Walk	*Simon Townson*
Bilsdale Circuit	*Malcolm Boyes*
Cal-der-Went Walk	*Geoffrey Carr*
Countryside Walks around Bradford	*Senior Wayfarers*
Countryside Walks around Leeds	*Ivan E. Broadhead*
Countryside Walks around Scarborough	*Malcolm Boyes*
Countryside Walks around York	*Ken Piggin*
Crosses Walk	*Malcolm Boyes*
The Derwent Way	*Richard C. Kenchington*
Ebor Way	*J. K. E. Piggin*
Eskdale Way	*Louis S. Dale*
Long Distance Walks—	
1. North York Moors and Wolds	*Tony Wimbush*
2. Yorkshire Dales	*Tony Wimbush & Allan Gott*
3. The Peak	*Tony Wimbush*
Lyke Wake Walk	*Bill Cowley*
Nidderdale Way	*J. K. E. Piggin*
Pennine Way	*Kenneth Oldham*
Six Dales Hike	*J. D. Burland*
Trans-Pennine Walk	*Richard Mackrory*
Walking in Bronte Country	*Ramblers' Association*
Walking in Craven Dales	*Colin Speakman*
Walking in Northern Dales	*Ramblers' Association*
Walking in the South Pennines	*Clifford Thompson*
Walking in Teesdale	*Keith Watson*
Walking in the Three Peaks	*Colin Speakman*
Walks From Your Car—	
Bilsdale and the Hambletons	*Ramblers' Association*
Eskdale and the Cleveland Coast	*Ramblers' Association*
Rosedale and Farndale	*Malcolm Boyes*
Walks in Lower Wharfedale	*Geoffrey White*
Walks in Nidderdale	*Geoffrey White*
Walks in Swaledale	*Geoffrey White*
Walks in Upper Wharfedale	*Michael Obst*
Walks in Wensleydale	*Geoffrey White*
Walks North of York	*Geoffrey White & Geoffrey Green*
Walks on the North York Moors	*Ramblers' Association*
Wayfarer Walks in the South Pennines	*Colin Speakman*
White Rose Walk	*Geoffrey White*
Wolds Way	*David Rubinstein*
Yoredale Way	*J. K. E. Piggin*

Send S.A.E. for current book list to Dalesman Books, Clapham, via Lancaster, LA2 8EB.